To Oria,

Many Blessings

Rau

Praise for *Cultivating Spirituality in Children*

Here is a wonderful immersion into the spiritual values we need within ourselves, so we may help nurture the children in our lives. Dr. Rosie Kuhn helps us live and share the values we so desperately want for our children and for the next generations to come. This little book, *Cultivating Spirituality in Children*, reminds us that the best thing we can do for children is to start with ourselves. It shares with us an achievable path of insight, and skills.—David Bennett author of *A Voice as Old as Time* & *Voyage of Purpose*

*****

"If you are an adult who lives or works with children, then I highly recommend reading this book.

Dr. Rosie Kuhn writes from the heart. Her work is powerful, thought-provoking and takes the reader on a transformational journey inward. By the end, it is clear why it's so important for parents to figuring out our own spirituality, so that we can serve as inspiration to our children.

This book raises our level of consciousness, and challenges us to think about what it is that children need from us.

I especially appreciated the level of vulnerability to which Dr. Kuhn was willing to go, which makes the book all the more touching and personal."

-     Valerie Davis-Rucker, MS, MBA, CLC

*****

"Any parent or person who works with children and is interested in cultivating an authentic, heart-centered relationship with them needs to read this book and put these 101 pieces of wisdom into practice!

Dr. Rosie Kuhn once again empowers us to acknowledge and be with our own humanness and vulnerability in a way that strengthens our ability to integrate our spiritual nature here on earth. By putting these 101 pieces of wisdom into practice you will not only be cultivating a child's spirituality, but you will also be freeing yourself from the bondage of the cultural baggage of what it means to be a parent and a caregiver." *Elizabeth J. Sabet PCC, ACSLC ,*

-   Executive Director of HOPE – Holistic Options for People Everywhere, and Mom

*****

The theme of this book — that the spiritual life of our children depends on the spiritual competency with which we live our own lives — sets the priorities correctly. A parent who ignores or distorts spirituality while taking the stance: *do as I say, not as I do*--is not going to effectively foster the spiritual life of their children.

The practices in this book enable parents, teachers or any adult to share their spirituality with children. It provides a guide for traveling a path together with our children, which cultivates a spiritual journey based on sharing joy, compassion and forgiveness. *David Lukoff Ph.D., Spiritual Competency Resource Center, www.spiritualcompetency.com*

*****

"Dr. Kuhn discusses an important, yet neglected area of parenting: spirituality and children. She raises some important questions about how best to raise children within a spiritual paradigm and context. Dr. Kuhn also suggests that we have as much to learn from our children regarding staying connected and open to the spiritual domain, and introduces a much needed discussion about this topic."

- *Shawn Katz, Ph.D., and Dad*

*****

"Dr. Rosie Kuhn has blessed us with her new book, *Cultivating Spiritual in Children: 101 Ways To Make Every Child's Spirit Soar. A* book overflowing with wisdom, Rosie teaches us that the best gift we can give our children, and grandchildren, is being the person you want them to be. It doesn't matter if you have children or not, Rosie offers ways to live our life in a way that is authentic while honoring that we are fallible human beings, whose world isn't always perfect. And that is okay... when this happens refer to Experience #31, and be okay with 'The Big Fat Be-With.' If we put even a few of these 101 life-altering suggestions into practice, we will change not only our own children and grandchildren, we will change our world!"

- *Cindy Griffith Author of Soul Soothers: Mini Meditations for Busy Lives*

*****

"The first inspiring and effective compilation of opportunities to live life to the fullest as parents, grandparents, guardians, children...and spiritual beings." Hagai Heshes MAPP, and Dad

*****

If you're at all concerned about how to best support and encourage spirituality in your children, or in any children who may be under your care, Dr. Rosie Kuhn has written the book for you! Make no mistake, though, as Dr. Kuhn makes clear, cultivating spirituality in children isn't all about what to preach — it is about walking the walk more than talking the talk. Whether we realize it or not, no amount of preaching will reach the mark when we're out of alignment with our own truth, values and principles. Dr. Kuhn encourages us to engage our own spirituality, and her

101 opportunities to practice provide ample ideas for doing just that, ultimately ensuring a more positive impact on our children's spiritual growth too. *A. Scott McCulloch, PhD MBA - Transpersonal/Transformational Coach, Thought Partner, Insight Facilitator, Founder of Tapintu*

Cultivating Spirituality
In Children

101 Ways To Make
Every Child's Spirit SOAR!

© 2015 by Rosie Kuhn, Ph.D.
First published in the United States by
The Paradigm Shifts Publishing Co.
PO Box 1637, Eastsound WA 98245
Cover design & Continuity Editing by Maureen O'Neill, at
On Fire Coaching.
(Fonts: Cover: Adobe Caslon Pro, Semi-bold Italics; Marker
Felt Phin; Text: Book Antiqua),
Edited by Jessica Ruby Hernandez, at Ruby Moon Healing
Arts.

Cover Photo by: The Picture People, Amherst, NY

ISBN: 978-0-9908151-1-2

Dedication

To Andrew Jacob Fesyk, my grandson,
who inspired the writing of this book.

Table of Contents

Something to Keep in Mind:

The human and spiritual developments process often comes with physical, emotional, and energetic sensations. Though these feelings may seem disorienting, uncomfortable and a little disconcerting at times, they are a natural and normal component of this journey.

Most of us avoid and ignore the self-discovery process because we are uncomfortable with being uncomfortable. Expanding your capacity to be with discomfort may be part of what transpires for you as you read this book.

Consider making sure you drink plenty of water and get plenty of rest, if and when you experience fatigue. And, consider enlisting the support of a Transformational Coach, a Spiritual Guide, a fellowship group for addiction recovery, ACISTE.org for spiritually transformative experiencers, friends, and family who can listen and hear you.

Most of all, practice extending loving kindness and compassion to yourself. I have no doubt you will be delighted with your experience at the completion of this journey.

Introduction

Children are spiritual beings who, just a short time ago, adventured into the world of humans. They enter our world already having a spiritual life. In their innocence, they have access to the wisdom and wonder of the world from which they came. They still enjoy relationships with the unseens: angels and guides, their devoted friends from the other side. They have the innate ability to connect with their Spirit-selves and the spiritual world, until they become more like the rest of us. When does that happen? When do they decide to forget their essential nature as Spirit-beings? How do we as grownups participate in this forgetting? This book is my answer to those questions."

Chapter 1

You Picked Up this Book – Terrific!

You are a grownup in search of ways to nurture children's spirituality. At the same time, you want to walk intentionally on your own spiritual path. I'm happy to say, this book is for you!

This book is written for grownups who are invested in introducing spiritual values to children – enough that they are willing to take a look at the words they, themselves speak, as well as the actions they take, and ask themselves: *Are my words and my actions in alignment with what I want for my children? Am I willing to take on practices that will not only cultivate awareness in me, but also shift my thoughts, my words and my actions, so that they are in alignment with my highest values and my highest contribution to my children's well-being?*

From the title of this book, you might expect to find specific lists of what our children need in order to develop spiritually. Instead, I offer you an opportunity to think bigger. I challenge you to be willing to look deeper for what children really need from you.

Until we grownups commit to cultivating spiritual competencies within ourselves, our children have no reason to believe a word we say. Our actions constantly speak louder than our words, either reflecting our fear-based thinking or mirroring our Divine knowing. And, as you already know, children take their lessons from who we are being, not from what we are saying.

We all pretend not to know when we act out of alignment with our principles, but in reality, we know immediately when we're not practicing our core truths. How do we pretend not to know? Why do we pretend not to know?

In order to step fully into helping children soar as Spirit beings, we have to first be willing to practice investigating, visiting, and enlivening our own deeply held spiritual principles. Then we must be willing to take up the practice of living into these principles. If we do this, children will inevitably follow our lead.

By opening to cultivating spirituality in ourselves, we bravely make ourselves available to practice whatever it takes to expand our own courage, faith and Self-trust. These practices are deeply humbling, and at the same time, nurture solid confidence within ourselves. By these practices, we develop a delightful sense of self-knowing and self-trust, which until now, have remained out of reach. We live into a life with less stress, greater ease, and a sweet ability to accept and live peacefully with what is.

Through these practices, we also become far more willing to be present in our children's lives, as the gift of their presence in our lives becomes very, very clear. If this is the kind of parent/stepparent/grandparent or guardian that you've dreamt of becoming– read on!

Chapter 2

The Rules Of Consensus Thinking

Conforming to the standards set out by culture, religion, government, education, society, and family, often requires that we deny and ignore our own internal reality, our soul or Spirit-self, if you will, for the sake of what we get, or hope to get, from blind allegiance to external power sources. In exchange for our loyalty and obedience, we expect to be rewarded with security, stability, status, and perhaps monetary gain. For those committed to serving God through religious practices, we expect to effortlessly pass through the gates of heaven.

However, few people actually experience the rewards of such service. Most of us inevitably realize that we've abdicated our souls – our Spirit-self, for the sake of allegiance to the promise-makers, not the promise-keepers. This is endemic in both Western and Eastern societies. We are in denial of that fact that, not only have we been willing participants in this process, but we are training our children to do the same.

From the moment we are born, we are immersed in a learning process, which, more often than not, teaches us to do what we are told to do. In childhood, most of us learn to think what we are taught to think and to ignore our own inner voice. We are taught to ignore our emotions, our bodies and their messages.

We also learn to deny our own personal needs and wants, for the sake of others' needs and desires – these *others* often include our schools, churches, governments, families, as well as friends. We train ourselves to follow fear-based thinking, which is at present, the consensus view of reality. When we have an original thought or creation, we usually do not follow it, as it would be dangerous to break with this consensus thinking.

We train ourselves to not only *ignore* our inner truth, but to buy into the lie that it isn't safe to trust it. In this way, we are banishing it for perhaps a lifetime, or, at least until it is safe to begin to question reality.

In essence, this is where each of us are today; vaguely aware of the existence of an inner ME (Miraculous Existence) that has thoughts, feelings, needs and wants, and at the same time, afraid to explore that inner-self, because we are convinced that the ramifications may be dire.

Chapter 3

Confused?

Most of us live with a nagging confusion, due to the fact that we are immersed in a reality where religion and spiritual traditions are touted as the bedrock of our society. As children, many of us were taught spiritual principles through religion. However, the majority of our religious institutions are systems governed by a hierarchy of authority that requires obedience to the rules and to those who enforce the rules. We then train ourselves to be vigilant to "doing it right" and "not doing it wrong". In so doing, we hope to avoid punishment, persecution, and damnation. As a result, the spiritual principles we were meant to live by were kicked to the curb.

We hear the words – "Think Differently," "Be the Exception," "Go for the Extraordinary," "Be Your Self". However, more often than not, the humiliation, ridicule, and ostracizing that is rampant, even within our elementary schools, convinces us to play small, and keep our ideas to ourselves. It's very confusing – especially to children.

Each of us grownups carries the wounding and trauma created through our own parents' confusion and inconsistencies: not walking their talk, not saying what they mean and not meaning what they say. Most of us, now as grownups, pretend that we aren't confused or challenged by these dilemmas. Rather than addressing our confusion, we, like our parents, ignore it, in hopes that sometime later in life, the questions will answer themselves.

In the meantime, we, perhaps unconsciously, are doing and saying just as our parents said and did. Though we sometimes catch ourselves in the act, rarely are we willing to make a change. And, like our parents, we hope that our children and grandchildren don't notice. The sad fact is, they *do* notice, and are deeply affected by the contradictions of our words and actions – just like we were and are today.

Here's the bottom line: as long as we continue to deny and avoid addressing our confusion and these obvious incongruities, we will continue to contribute to our own personal suffering, and to our children's suffering.

With that said...

Chapter 4

The End of Confusion

Few of us willingly choose to question reality unless we have some kind of a catalyst that sets us up for the inevitable instant when we find it untenable to live as we have been living. For some, it's a midlife crisis, where life is void of meaning and the questioning of reality cannot be circumvented any longer. For others, it may be a cataclysmic event- earthquake, hurricane, a diagnosis of a terminal illness, a loss of career, or a loss of a most important being- through death, divorce, or irresponsibility.

At some point, the angst and agony of clinging obediently to a life that has been void of the promised rewards will be abandoned. This is when one willingly chooses to question the belief systems of their family and culture, in search of the answers to questions, which have remained unanswerable within their current reality.

This search for personal truth and meaning usually leads one on a personal quest. It is a time of unraveling the confusion. It is a time to discern one's values and choose how to align one's actions with personal values and truths. It is a time to risk losing the safety and security of the known world, separating out the threads of stories, parables, and rules set out by an authority, in hopes of finding clear answers. It is a time of discernment and choice-making, empowering oneself to think, feel, and act upon one's own truth.

Generally, this journey requires the inclusion of a power greater than the authority found in religion, government, or any other organization on Earth. It begins to crack the 3D reality to include that which is invisible. It allows for experimentation, to not only call upon the support of a Divine Wisdom, but to allow the receiving of this wisdom.

Carefully, incrementally, we take steps away from our fear-based decision-making. And just as incrementally, we begin taking steps based on our essential knowing and deep truths. We willingly begin to discern relative truths from absolute truths, then take actions based on our direct findings.

At some point in this process, we realize that we are on a spiritual quest, and are cultivating a relationship with our higher selves – our Spirit-selves. We are developing a quality relationship with our spirituality that will not match any earthly relationship we have experienced thus far.

This journey is wrought with dangerous choice-points. As we navigate the thousands of belief systems and practices in the world, it is extremely challenging to stay true to our unique and individual design. While desiring to get it right, and at the same time get it safely and easily, we may immerse ourselves in a set of values and truths that are similar to ours, but still not ours.

It is not uncommon for individuals on such a journey to decide to join new spiritual or religious organizations, feeling the desire for safety within consensus and community. However, to do so often pulls us into similar patterns of our original relationship with authority and religion, leaving behind the desire for fulfillment within our own inner-authority, i.e., our unique spirit. Cultivating authority from within is the quintessential practice for reaching the fulfillment of our human spirit.

These experimentations with other religious and spiritual traditions may just be weigh-stations to collect oneself and one's thoughts. Inevitably though, like Buddha, Krishna, Jesus, and other truly significant spiritual teachers, we *all* will have to take the road less traveled - the one intended and fashioned only by us, and only for us.

Chapter 5

Let's Talk About Spirituality

Theoretically, spirituality is the cultivation of a deep and authentic relationship with our Divinity – our creator and all of creation. Spirituality is also each individual's process of revealing the ever present, ever deeper, richer layers of unity, sometimes referred to as *Oneness With All That Is*. This Divinity is the life force within all beings, and can only be fully known through direct, personal experience. Through applied dedication, we can begin to curiously explore, experiment and discover the truest relationship with our Spiritual-self.

Religious and spiritual traditions provide us with principles and practices, which elevate awareness and support conscious living. Additionally, many require an adherence to rules that govern moral and ethical standards.

Spirituality, on the other hand, is a personal endeavor to develop the ability to self-govern, based on one's own truth and integrity. Cultivating spiritual competence is a journey towards intentionally finding and claiming one's own unique relationship with Spirit. Only through this personal and very intimate process can each of us actualize our fullest expression of our essential nature, as Divine Beings.

Cultivating spirituality in children requires that those of us committed to such a practice begin by first nurturing our own relationship with our Spirit-self. By doing so, we become spiritual pioneers, and our children will be inspired to walk in our footsteps.

Chapter 6

Welcome To Your Possibility

Every one of us is endowed with an innate quest for meaning and understanding of the unknown and invisible world within. We long to experience this "something" we know to be true, yet is beyond logical and rational reason. Our deepest desire is to be an expression of the *sacred*. We may not know what that *sacred* is until we have the direct experience of it, but our deep longing for it inevitably brings us onto a path of self-reflection, self-realization and self-actualization.

We listen to, we sit with, and we gain guidance from those who have had direct experience with this invisible world. As much as we'd like to believe that it is enough to trust *them* and their experience, it is only through our own direct experience with the unexplainable world that we can truly and fully engage in a spiritual relationship with the Divine.

Consciously experimenting, exploring and discovering who we are, as Spirit within the circumstances of our human being, is the greatest gift we can give our children; in fact, it is imperative to their survival and the survival of our Earth. It is essential that we build this safe haven for our children, one within which they can know themselves, and thrive within their own incredible innate wisdom. We are all children nonetheless, and we are all ready to experience the delight of our own being. Welcome to your possibility!

Chapter 7

My Own Spiritual Path

As a child, I was often confused watching my parents be grownups. They were good people, yet I noticed that they sometimes swore, lied, cheated, and acted in unloving ways. Their actions often contradicted what they preached to us, and what we were taught in the Catholic Church. It became obvious to me, through my youthful eyes that, based on their actions and words, they were most likely going to go to Hell!

It did not make sense that most of the grownups I knew, including priests and nuns, acted in ways that were contrary to what they preached. In my child mind, this tangled the threads of my absolute knowing with filaments of doubt regarding the rules of living on Earth. There must be something I didn't understand, something besides going to confession and doing penance, which allowed people to enter the gates of Heaven, even though they were sinners.

I knew, without a doubt, that there was Divinity everywhere, in everything, always. However, the outside world reflected something that caused me doubt and uncertainty. I decided it wasn't safe to trust my inner knowing. In order to be safe, in order to get along in the world, I chose to move my trust to the authority and power in the world outside of me.

Chapter 8

The Beginning of the End

It was when I was six years old, in the first grade at Sacred Heart School, that I began my religious instructions. I was following in the footsteps of my five older siblings, and I could not wait to fulfill my greatest desire – to go to Catholic School, so I could become even more connected to God and Jesus than I already was.

Sister Mary Denata, my first grade teacher, began by telling us how God was all seeing, all knowing, and all powerful. Furthermore, she taught that this God was also an angry, punishing God – nothing like the One I knew as always lovingly there for me.

Shortly thereafter, came the lessons regarding sin and the punishment that comes along with sinning – inevitably going to Purgatory or to Hell.

After hearing Sister Mary Denata's version of truth about God and sin, everything changed. As this sweet, pure, budding, enthusiastic Catholic, I realized, with confusion and horror, that I was probably committing sins and didn't even know it. And, because God was all seeing, all knowing, all powerful, *and* angry when disobeyed, he had certainly caught me in the act of my sinning, and Hell would be my inevitable punishment. Through this version of truth, I grasped that I was guilty, and should be full of shame, just by virtue of being me.

I was only six, and could not conceive how to be me without committing sins. How do I protect my innocence from this cruel and uncaring religious reality that I was now entering? I imagined that, for the rest of my life, I would need to be vigilant against any possible failings, because God would know, and God would punish!

Don't ask me how I knew what to do, but in order to protect this pure-self, I hid her away in the deepest, most inner recesses of my being, where she would never be harmed or betrayed. This was the moment of my first shattering.

Chapter 9

When I was 17

When I was 17, immersed fully into the Catholic Doctrine, I questioned the truth of the Catholic Church. *Why am I always asking for mercy? Why was I not allowed to talk to God directly? Is there such a place as Hell? Why do I need to go to confession when I haven't done anything wrong? Why do I have suffer to demonstrate my worthiness? What happened to unconditional love?*

When I needed guidance the most, I couldn't get the attention of any adult to help me unravel my confusion. There was no grownup support to empower me to think for myself about what I needed to think about in order to live life truly rooted in spirituality and faith. Through angst and anguish, I came to the conclusion that I needed to rid myself of the hypocrisy, pretense, and confusion of the life I was living as a Catholic. I threw religion out the window. This was a second shattering.

This choice to leave the Catholic Church, and everything related to religion, caused my parents to furiously reject me. I didn't care. My life laid in the balance; I was tormented and alone, and for the first time in my life, I seriously considered suicide.

Not knowing who or what to believe, I made the choice to become what I call an *atheistic agnostic*. And, for the next twenty years, I lived, as best I could, in love, in the beauty of nature, and in kindness, as I turned my back on all of what religion offered. In my mid-thirties, all of that changed.

Chapter 10

Returning

As a therapist in Nova Scotia, working in the field of addiction, I was amazed to realize that people within the recovering community had something I didn't have. Through their AA and NA fellowships, individuals who were fully committed to recovering their lives were cultivating a deep, powerful, and authentic relationship with their higher power (as they defined him/her/it). They lived in faith, voluntarily suspending all beliefs that they could fix their problems by themselves. They surrendered their "stinking thinking" patterns and their old survival strategies to their higher power, as well. They learned how to accept what they could not change. They had serenity; I did not.

Through the witnessing of such clear results, I saw that I needed to reconsider my former decision regarding religion and spirituality. I came to decide that I wanted what they had, and I wanted it *enough* to cultivate the courage and faith to step onto the path to waking up.

I didn't quite know where to begin. All I knew was that how I was being in my life wasn't working for me. I was miserable and dysfunctional in all of my relationships, and I had nowhere to turn for solace and peace. Yes, I was a therapist – as sick as they come, and, my recovering clients gave me a glimpse into the possibility of another way.

Facing the insanity of all that I unwittingly created, I began reading books on Co-dependency, Adult Children of Alcoholics, and then read the book: *A Course In Miracles*. The work of self-healing was grueling and demanding. But, by taking one arduous step at time, one day at a time, I slowly and deliberately recovered fragments of myself that I had buried long ago.

What's more, I realized something so horrendous, I could hardly stand being inside my own skin. When I was 17, and rejected religion, I rejected that which is at the very heart of my being, and truth be told, is at the heart of every single religion: The direct experience of knowing union with the Divine Presence. Yup! This is what saints, gurus, and spiritual teachers talk about – their personal and direct experience of God!

Realizing this, I dug into the practice of ridding myself of my defenses, my resistance, my willfulness. As I did so, I discovered something beautiful – a Divine partnership was unfolding. It was the reunifying of my smaller-self with my Divine-Self.

Today, I'm humbled by the realization that my path over these past thirty years miraculously reunited me with my child-self and the absolute knowing that I experienced in the innocence of my childhood.

Nowadays there isn't a day that goes by that I'm not in communion with my Divine-Self. In fact, this is the most important companion in my life. I now know that this relationship will never end, and will never cease to bring phenomenal love, delight, and serenity into my life.

** If you are interested in the full story, my book: _The Unholy Path of a Reluctant Adventurer_ (2011), reveals it all.

Chapter 11

Coping with the Shatterings

The specific shatterings that I've shared, happened within the context of religion. Shatterings come about through any number of contexts: abuse, neglect, betrayal, accidents, and loss, to name just a few.

Most of us, before or around the age of six, experience a traumatic and life-shattering event. It is a moment when each of us comes face-to-face with an unexpected and devastating happening. Something is said, something is done, something occurs, and in the blink of an eye, we come to realize a new truth about ourselves: that we are not safe as the innocent, sweet beings we have been. This moment heralds the loss of fearlessness and innocence.

This is one of the most isolating event of our young lives. We cannot share this moment, or what we decided, based on this moment, because, firstly, we don't have a language for the experience, or for our feelings; and, secondly, most likely grownups will either not believe us, or they will not take us seriously.

In this moment, we decide that no one is trustable or trustworthy. We are lost and alone against the world.

It is important to note that, it isn't the context of these shatterings that is significant, but what underlies the context. Shatterings occurs whenever we are exposed to something so contrary to our innocent perspective that our absolute trust is rocked. Suddenly, everything we know is wrong. Our inexperienced version of truth is obliterated, an amnesia sets in, and our essential-selves are forgotten. We come to decide that we can no longer depend upon, or trust, what we knew we could trust just moments before.

Although, this shattering occurs within seconds, every adult I've spoken with remembers how traumatic it was to choose, as a child, to hide away their innocent-self. They also remember that they made a promise to return and reunite with this pure essence-self. As grownups, they struggle with making good on that promise, and, at the same time, knowing their soul's survival is at stake.

Like any good novel, stage play, or movie, before the return and rescue can take place, the plot has to thicken; more characters come on the scene to make things more interesting and adventurous. So, who is it that will come to our rescue?

Chapter 12

Enter the Ego

Let's review: We've realized that we were just little innocent beings with no power and no trust; we didn't know what the heck we were doing. We get that we couldn't trust anyone to listen to us, to understand us, or to willingly support us in our hour of need. We felt alone, confused, vulnerable and desperate. Conclusion made: "Survival" is the best we can hope for right now. SIGH!

Then, out of the blue, like a Genie from a bottle, we hear a voice, inside our heads; one that hasn't made itself known before this moment. This voice whispers, "You can trust me. I will keep you safe. Listen only to me and I won't let you down!" How fortuitous that this being should come along, just when we needed it most.

This voice says that it is committed to our survival. It tells us that it knows how to work with the reality that surrounds us – especially with grownups who hold our fate in their hands. This choice-maker is different than the one we relied on in our innocence. The price we pay for our survival, however, is that we have to promise our allegiance to it for the rest of our lives. A small price to pay for survival. Though it appears to be life-giving, we may have just sold our soul to the devil.

It isn't the devil we've just met. It's the start of a beautiful relationship with our ego-self.

We come to trust this internal being more than any other person in our sweet little lives. In fact, from this moment on, we are in total service to never letting our ego-self down. And, we don't even know we are doing this!

The good news is that inevitably, somewhere in our grownup lives, we come to see how this choice-maker, the ego, betrays us. Another shattering will occur, in support of this happening, and we will have the opportunity to think differently, in service to something greater than our ego-self. Call it, perhaps, a mid-life crisis.

Yes, that is the good news!

Chapter 13

Subduing the Naturally Occurring Happily Ever After

Each of us, at one time or another, have had to reorient ourselves from a world of innocence and unconditional love, to getting "real" in the world. This requires learning important new shoulds and shouldn'ts, and that there are people and things we need to be afraid of. We are taught, wittingly or unwittingly, the rules of who to judge and how to hate.

We are so young when our first shattering occurs, and life has suddenly become dangerous. Our new six year-old choice-maker – our ego, immediately sets about creating a set of strategies to keep us safe. Our undertaking is to stop being spontaneous, curious, and trusting, and start being sharply vigilant for possible danger and vulnerability. This is the end of what I call *the naturally occurring happily ever after.*

Whether abused, neglected, abandoned, or betrayed, all children learn to assess situations in nano-seconds for potential danger. We learn to take on guilt and shame, humiliation and embarrassment. We learn to defend and protect what is ours and what we want to be ours. We have given up our essential selves in order to survive within the fear-based, consensus view of reality. We believe it is imperative to protect what little is left of our identity.

Researchers report that 70% of our thinking life is made up of negative thoughts. This habitually negative thinking constantly alerts us to the possibility of worst-case scenarios. To one degree or another, we constantly live in fear.

As we mature, we continually develop more sophisticated survival strategies that we believe will maintain our invulnerability. We focus exclusively on how to survive and suppress our inborn innocence and our natural communion with the wonder-filled worlds beyond this world. So many of us forget how to play and create. We stopped being effortlessly present with our angels and guardian beings. Exuberance and delight are secreted away, with our deepest, purest, most sincere promise to return at such time that it is safe do so.

Chapter 14

Enter Spiritual Evolution

In essence, spiritual evolution is the flip side of our initial trauma. It begins with flashes of awareness of the distinct voice of our made-up choice-maker. This voice previously seemed like our own, and seemed as if it had been with us for eternity. We slowly recall our natural innocence, before all the shatterings and traumas we've endured; before handing over our power to the ruthless choice-maker, the ego.

Spiritual evolution can begin with an event as traumatic as our original trauma. It too creates a pathway, but this time, it opens us to the possibility to fulfill our promise from long ago. We begin to realize that we are not what we decided when we were five or six: powerless, unworthy, insignificant. We begin to remember our essential Self.

Spiritual evolution is the process of opening to remembering our innocence, our fearless grace, and the truth that we are an essential expression of the Divine.

The original trauma separated us from our Source and the knowing of our true nature: love, joy, innocence, fearlessness, and more. As grownups, we are now consciously and intentionally able to choose to separate from the choice-maker we created at six years old – the one that convinced us that there was something terribly wrong with us, and that we didn't deserve anything without first proving our worth. This is the beginning and the end.

Chapter 15

Life Is Different Now

Until now, trauma has served as our best catalyst for waking up. Until our generation arrived, this was the best we humans could hope for. We had no other framework, so we lived from one breakdown (traumatic experience) to the next. But maybe, just maybe, we are ready to shift our perspective.

It is no secret that the level of consciousness now accessible actually empowers us to cease and desist creating trauma in our children, in ourselves, and in the world. We are beginning to understand that it is no longer necessary to breakdown in order to breakthrough.

Each of us possesses the innate intelligence and power to design our everyday life as a reflection of what we desire. Simply *knowing* this isn't enough though. Our insights and realizations aren't going to make it happen. What's required is that we walk our talk.

The first step is to build our courage so that it becomes the bridge from our fear-based resistance to the new experience of direct knowing. Step-by-daring-step, we can move across this bridge to experience for ourselves the Divine process of developing spiritually. We practice re-membering and re-embodying the original union, our non-dual state, as it was before our six-year-old self forgot who we were in service to survival.

Chapter 16

Rebooting Our Intelligence

Until now, we have all willingly participated in the old paradigm. Our mind's usual, passive response "Well, that's just the way it is," doesn't work anymore. As we cultivate our awareness, we are all waking up and becoming conscious of the fact that we are not the roles we play. We are Spirit-beings within these human forms, which we have, until now, identified as "me."

As we open to our new potential, we willingly reboot our innate intelligence. During breakdowns and traumatic events, rather than acting as if we are alone and powerless, we can practice allowing wisdom and intelligence to once again emerge within us. We allow our whole self to be present. And, we can directly experience ourselves expanding towards the full expression of our potentiality. This is what we long for in ourselves and for our children.

Honoring Our Nemesis

Inevitably, as we re-engage our intelligence, we realize that, what we considered to be the ruthless choice-maker – the ego, was actually that part of our humanity that has endured lifetime after lifetime of horrific and traumatic experiences, which did not end in our favor. Our ego-self has lived and died from within the unbreakable mandate that survival is all there is. Its sole mission has been to keep us alive. When surviving is the best one can hope for, thriving is a ridiculous concept.

Now, with our newly discovered capacity to evolve consciously, we can be grateful that our ego has kept us alive long enough to move us towards a more expanded reality, one focused on thriving. We can forgive its ruthlessness, and then openly express our compassion for its desire to protect us at all cost from any potential failing.

This moment reflects all the lifetimes we've encountered, all the courage we've mustered, all the trust to live one more day, the compassion for all that it took to choose to choose what we chose, and to honor ourselves for taking on this noble adventure as a human being. This aspect of ourselves, our ego, is responsible for bringing us here to this moment beyond survival, when we are ready for something more – something unfathomable, something worth living for – something worth dying for.

Chapter 17

How Do We Help Nurture And Sustain The Divine Knowing Of Our Children?

As a grandmother of a 4 year-old grandson, I ask myself the question: *How do I need to be, as parent of adult children, and as a grandparent, to nurture and sustain a spiritual orientation in my children and grandson?*

I admit that I did a poor job of providing spiritual sustenance for my children when they were young; therefore, I cannot draw on my own personal experience to answer that question. So, I sit here, wondering and discerning: How do I *be* in my own life, so that I can cultivate an environment that is spiritually enriching for all children and for myself? How do I allow the original Divine knowing that is present within all children to be continually nurtured and nourished? How do any of us rekindle that presence of Divine knowing, which was once all we knew to exist?

Because of the enormous amount of information and wisdom humanity has accumulated and disseminated over the ages, from the East and from the West, in this current lifetime, we have a new capability to evolve consciously. This has never been true until now. We now realize that over centuries, we humans have been expanding our capacity to think and to choose intentionally. In this current moment, as a parent, step-parent, guardian, or grandparent, how do we choose to utilize this inconceivable gift – to think and to choose intentionally, opening to evolving ourselves and our children?

Chapter 18

Dive Into Wonder

Extraordinary metaphysical phenomena happen every day here on planet Earth. Most of us have already, or will experience one or more mystical and transformative occurrences in our life. These include experiences of unexplained immediate knowing; wild synchronicities; out of body events; whispers and visions of friends or relatives that have passed; and many, many more.

We often choose to ignore or justify these experiences in order to sidestep acknowledging that they are real or significant. We diligently train ourselves to pretend they never happened. But, over the course of a lifetime, the accumulated evidence builds and points to a new and expansive view of our world that calls out to be identified and recognized.

These unexplainable experiences act as our personal trail of breadcrumbs- indicators that something, or someone is calling- but who or what? And how? These flashes of Divine clues lead us to curiosity and to wonder. This is a good thing!

Everyday, hundreds of organizations related to spiritually transformative experiences, and other non-ordinary phenomena, are birthing themselves on the internet. Data provided through personal interviews, as well as more "scientific" collection of data, strongly indicates a much greater reality than the one we believe to be living in.

With this ever-growing body of data available at our fingertips, when our children share experiences that seem beyond reason, we grownups have an opportunity to nurture their wonder and curiosity, rather than snuff it out by accusing them of fabrication and lying. If we choose to take their hand and step with them into the delightful presence of life that is beyond explanation, beyond the life-sucking norm of consensus reality, we offer our children a vast experience of life.

Chapter 19

Turning Inward

As I ponder how to bring spirituality into the lives of children, especially into my grandson's life, an inescapable question arises within me: *What must I learn and practice before I can teach spiritual principles and guidelines to the children in my life?*

I notice how I and many other grownups repeatedly turn to alcohol, drugs, medications, and other mind-numbing activities to drown out what consensus reality calls *nonsensical* thinking. I've become mindfully aware of the various methods available to corral chaotic thinking, irritability, pain, and suffering. It's just so much easier to ignore, distract, avoid, and deny challenges and confusions. Shopping, sex, gambling, complaining, worry and work are so much more valued, though they do not empower us in the midst of daunting circumstances. They do not support us in generating wisdom, acceptance, forgiveness, or compassion. They don't help – they just give us a bit of space between us and our challenges.

What if there is another, simpler way to be with life, which would help us make sense of it, and be less afraid of the way things are? What if there exists a more compassionate, less painful and self-damaging way to be with life's everyday challenges?

Perhaps, like the philosophers say, "The answer lies within."

If we practice turning inward again and again, trusting ourselves and diving deep, we can access a rich reservoir of ever-present, internal support. When doing so, we may be repeatedly surprised at our own abilities to empower and support ourselves. It is actually easy to learn to be present to the deep sense of pain we've been carrying, for perhaps lifetimes. We can remember all the evidence and experiences that now disprove the belief that, "There is no one and nothing out there that can help me." Through our own direct experience, we can cultivate a resilience, and return to trusting our own knowing. Through this process, we discover for ourselves how effortless it can be to eliminate the need for mind-numbing choices.

We teach children by example. Our new way of being demonstrates how they too can be present to their own internal support system, reminding them how to access a universe of support that is always there for them. We can empower and support them in remembering that they can rely on their own truths, and ensure that they don't feel the need to turn to unhealthy ways of being, as we have before them.

Most children have few compassionate guides to walk alongside them as they explore life, nature, and the myriad of extraordinary experiences that only make sense within a spiritual context. This absence of spiritual partnership for children is a big problem; one which I believe contributes to so many of our troubles in our world.

We can't protect our children from life, because they, like us, came here to experience life to its fullest, in human form. But we can choose to be a thinking partner for them, and to point them to tools that they can access while being with the good stuff *and* the not so good stuff, without scaring the bejeesus out of them. We can choose!

Chapter 20

Let's Put Simplicity Back into Spirituality

These days, my work in the world is to cultivate awareness in everyone – empowering them to awaken into greater consciousness and wisdom, in themselves and their children. My intention with this set of 101 practices is to put powerful simplicity back into spirituality.

I absolutely and unequivocally know that this is easier said than done, and that it requires all of us women and men to put on our adult undies, and be accountable, be responsible, and to truly take a stand for our personal truth. We need to do this for the sake of the fulfillment of our human spirit, and for that of our children.

Each of us knows instinctively what is true and life-generating. We also know instinctively what is untrue, false, and fear-based. We know how to choose to act in alignment with our truths, and how to choose in alignment with our fears. We can feel it deep within our bodies, physically and emotionally, when we act in alignment with our truths, or our fears. We assess the degree to which we want what we desire, and the degree to which we want to avoid what is undesirable. And, then we choose. Simple, right?

Though we make spirituality about right and wrong, good and bad, it really has nothing to do with that, . . . really. It only has to do with knowing what your highest truth is and acting in alignment with that. Bottom line: It's only a matter of stopping every thought and action that is not in alignment with your highest truth! Just stop doing what doesn't work, to bring a sense of well-being into your life.

Most of us ignore the whole subject of spirituality, hoping our children will get it from someone else: from Hebrew classes, Catechism, Sunday school, or other religious instruction. In this way, we can avoid dealing with the confusion and the angst of having to choose which principles and practices we wish to encourage in our children; we can avoid the discomfort of being confronted with what is *really* true for us, which may not be true for others; and we can avoid the potential conflict of going against the grain of those who will disagree with us.

However, when we become parents and grandparents, we are given an opportunity to grow ourselves up into adults, into the kind of person we want our children to be. We can choose to either parent the same way our parents did (likely through guilt and shame), or we can choose to choose differently.

Ideally, we will all inevitably choose to practice what we preach and to walk our talk. We will inevitably use our intelligence to think about life, what's true for us, and what we want to share with the world, through our own lives, and through our children. In doing so, we can truly begin to teach our children the spiritual competencies that will put them on a path to playfulness, creativity, faith, and fulfillment.

For me, alongside playfulness, creativity, faith, and fulfillment, I want my grandson to never have to forget his innocence; and that his faithful angels and companions are always present – he is never alone. I want him to talk with these companions as easily as he talks with his stuffed animals, his cars, and his parents. I want him to continue to remember that sometimes, when life gets scary and makes no sense, there *is* a greater wisdom at work. That, though the circumstances that present themselves appear to reflect failure or incompetence on his part, he is so much more than what this moment is challenging him with.

I want all children to take the higher ground when they see the higher ground; to think differently, looking within; strengthening the ability to *expand their awareness and consciousness* to include something that hasn't yet revealed itself, yet is trustworthy.

I want children of all ages to have the opportunity to cultivate a personal relationship with the Divine, in the way that works best for them, and to know the value of such a relationship. This allows all sorts of practices, which allows the Spirit-Self to be accessible and relevant to their particular perspectives and desires.

To summarize:

In his book *The Secret Spiritual World of Children* (2003), Tobin Hart points to the fact that as adults, we often thwart our children's innate wisdom, through our actions, our talking, and through our rules and regulations – forgetting that our children most likely have a closer relationship to the Divine than we grown-ups remember of our own growing up years.

In choosing to be parents, we create opportunities to show our children what it might look like to live in our own truth – literally walk our talk. This is a very powerful practice.

Having the consciousness to courageously investigate and examine our beliefs and to practice ways of being that align with our highest desires – isn't this the crux of what we are wanting to generate in our children?

Parenting provides an opportunity to partake in the evolution of consciousness of our children and our children's children. As grownups, we have the opportunity to parent all children in a way that nourishes thriving. All grownups function as guides and supports, one way or another. We can choose!

We are always, always, always opening to our highest values and highest truths, as we know them to be. What follows are 101 everyday opportunities to consider what those highest truths are; then to practice opening to those values, *before* teaching or preaching. This is only in alignment with supporting our children's Spirit to soar.

Chapter 21

Preflight Checklist:
Preparing Our Children for Takeoff

Before pilots and their planes are cleared for takeoff, they go through rigorous training and impeccable inspection of their plane to ensure safety, competence, and comfort. The pilot doesn't take flight until each item is checked off!

As parents, grandparents, and guardians, we are the ground crew for our young fledgling pilots, preparing them for the ride of their lives. We provide them with experiences and training that either support the development of intelligence, wisdom, and courage to fly solo, or keeps them grounded in fear and self-doubt. We encourage them to trust themselves, to know their fullest potential, and to respect themselves and their bodies. Or, we limit their ability to fly, through our own self-limiting beliefs.

We give our children both roots and wings: roots, so that they know their ground of being, and we give them wings to soar above limiting thinking. This allows them to freely explore the unlimited potentiality of the Universe. They need both, and you and I are the ground crew that makes it all possible.

Use this Preflight Checklist of practices for yourself and for all children. This offers you a way to center yourself and to bring your actions into alignment with your core values. You can practice sitting comfortably, becoming grounded, and allowing your actions to come solely from your convictions. In this way, both you and the children of the world are cleared for takeoff!

☐ Make the choice to be your children's Ground Crew. With your convictions and dedication, you are preparing them with everything required to get them off the ground. As their thinking partner, they will soar beyond the clouds.

☐ Do the work to get clear on your own convictions: What do you know to be true, *enough* that you align your actions with your words?

☐ Begin to question consensus reality, and consider rejecting what doesn't align with your values and convictions.

☐ Notice any judgments and beliefs that come from fear, and which limit the potentiality of takeoff and soaring.

☐ Be mindful of your thoughts, beliefs, assumptions, and expectations, and let go of any blocks to living in your highest truth. This will effortlessly allow your children to soar in their highest truth, for their highest good.

☐ Live as if you lack nothing in this moment. Let go of "Not Enough." Release the need for more time, more space, more power, more control – more anything. In doing so, your children will begin to grow into their natural capacity to thrive, free of anxiety and worry.

☐ When lost, unsure, or in doubt, request guidance from above – the flight tower – for there are those who have a much more expansive view of reality than you do working as the ground crew. Many of these wise beings are unseen, but nevertheless available for support and guidance.

☐ Defer your wisdom, your knowing, your truth and your values to no one.

Ready for Takeoff?

101 Ways to Make
Every Child's Spirit SOAR!

Experience #1

Opening to This Spiritual Journey

Wrapping our heads around the concept of spirituality is challenging enough, let alone, how to explain it to children. Possibilities are overwhelming: Heaven, hell; God, no God; Life after death; East vs. West; Angels and Demons. I want to ignore the whole subject!

At the same time, I know I would be remiss as a responsible grownup if I ignore the spiritual life of my children. I am willing to take a chance, because something wonderful might come of this!

Perhaps, just through the practice of observing how I *be* me, I'll see aspects of a spiritual life that has gone unrecognized and unlived, but is still within me, somewhere. Perhaps this will be a new beginning of something beautiful!

Experience # 2

Opening to Trusting Myself

Before I can truly trust others, I have to trust that I can trust myself.

As I practice noticing when I trust others over myself, I gain opportunities to trust myself instead. I practice deferring to no one outside of me and honoring my own innate knowing.

Experience #3

Opening to Developing a Relationship with ME (Miraculous Existence)

My sense of Self is founded on how I experience myself, not on how others experience me. Developing a relationship with the inner ME requires the practice of making time to be with my Self; it cannot happen any other way. By engaging in this practice, not only am I getting to know myself, but I am also cultivating self-appreciation and self-respect.

Experience #4

Opening to Respecting ME & My Voice

To trust my own experience requires that I practice having the courage to stand up for my thoughts and my truths, speak them clearly, and be with the consequences no matter what. In so doing, I realize a degree of self-respect I've never thought possible.

Experience #5

Opening to Experiencing
My Humanity to the Fullest

Being human takes a willingness to dive into that which wants to be experienced and expressed through me. When I practice surrendering my resistance, the art of life effortlessly manifests from within. My unique Divine Design blossoms into its own natural expression.

Experience #6

Opening to Clarifying
My Intentions and Convictions

For much of my life, I've lived according to the views and the beliefs of the people around me. I've handed my authority over to this consensus reality and abdicated my power. Hypnotized, I've lost all real connection to my own thoughts and feelings, and to my own needs and wants. I'm appalled at the degree to which I do not know myself.

As I'm coming out of the trance, I see that up until now, my highest intentions have been in service to survival. This ensured that I was accepted and approved of, and not rejected, humiliated, or shunned.

I see now how focusing only on survival was an act of self-betrayal. Without a real sense of me, I allowed myself to become just a part of the ebb and flow of consensus reality. Do I know who I am? Do I know what I want? Am I enough? Are my convictions strong enough and clear enough to keep me from falling back into the trance?

Discipline, commitment, and devotion come only through conviction. Convictions are strong beliefs wrapped up with a passionate presence. These convictions can be ignored, but not denied.

Without strong convictions, I will never be courageous enough to be committed enough to be devoted enough to truly know myself and to live into what I stand for. When I am unshakable and my convictions are undisputable, discipline takes on the nature of child's play.

I practice noticing what I think and what I feel about my life. I practice being curious about what I want. I question the degree to which I'm fulfilled in the life I'm giving myself. I sense deeper into myself for my truest convictions. Then, and only then, can I begin to make strides towards a more fulfilling and joyous life for me and for my children.

Experience #7

Opening to Cultivating Peace

I notice how I use irritation as a way to push others away in order to get "peace." It's not working.

I practice seeing when my irritation is based on a desire to avoid connection. I practice stretching my ability to be present in a way that allows me to enjoy the way that it is.

When I need solitude and peace, I practice asking for it in a way that preserves and sustains respectful acceptance of myself and others.

Experience #8

Opening to Truth and Humility

When I make a mistake and then I tell a lie about it, I dishonor myself and the people I am lying to.

When I practice telling the truth about my mistakes, I discover and begin to experience who I am in my humanness. I can then humbly acknowledge that I am not beyond failing to be perfect.

Experience #9

Opening to Patience

Sometimes I push to move things forward, thinking it's time to see results, but nothing moves. I feel stuck and frustrated. I don't know or understand what is stopping me.

By practicing patience, and allowing Divine Timing to unfold, I realize something is incubating, and that the time for action has yet to arrive. In doing so, I waste less time and energy judging myself as incompetent and unworthy of the task. I relax, take a breath, and patiently allow Divine Guidance to share with me what is mine to do now.

Experience #10

Opening to Intimacy

Too often, for the sake of pride and the desire to appear invulnerable, I avoid opportunities to share with others some of the challenges I face in my life. When sharing myself with others, I can choose to feel humiliated or I can choose to feel humbled. I practice being open and courageously sharing myself with others, whom I trust, for the sake of revealing more of me to me. Into Me See.

Experience #11

Opening to Surrender

What I believed to be true in the past is different today. It's crazy-making sometimes to be living in the moment and to live in the unfolding mystery.

I practice giving up ways of being that worked for me in the past but don't work for me in this moment. I practice surrendering to my Divine unfolding, letting go of any interpretation that is no longer aligning with this moment, in this moment.

Experience #12

Opening to Persistence and Resilience

It's unbearable and unendurable sometimes to suffer the anguish and pain of the internal archeological excavation of the authentic expression of my life. Then, Eureka! The mother lode is revealed and the thrill of the exploration has been renewed.

Persisting with calm patience, I willingly allow the process to move at its Divine Pace. Unwearyingly sitting in the midst of the remnants and relics of my life, I practice trusting that the treasure of such an expedition will be revealed to me in the right time and space.

Experience #13

Opening to My Higher Values

My principles, values, and perspective are sometimes different from those of my friends and family. Now and again, opening to a greater good, I have to choose based on what others want. This requires that I choose to look inside for values that serve a higher ME, which include others.

Perhaps, there is a value that can be served without feeling as though I am sacrificing, suffering, or settling. While sitting in deep listening with myself, I practice discerning what that value is, then shift my perceptions and actions and opening to that.

I practice noticing how I choose what I choose, and I use my choice-making muscles to choose differently.

Experience #14

Opening to Defying My Defiance

My child often acts out in defiant ways. No matter what I do or say, she continues to resist my authority. I feel like I'm the child and she thinks she's the boss of me!

However, when I quiet myself and my thoughts, I practice allowing a greater wisdom to be present with me. I ask myself: what part of me perhaps invites in the defiance; what part of me is defiant, maybe even a defiant parent, and how is my defiant child a teacher for me? What can I possibly learn from such behavior?

By allowing myself to sit with these uncomfortable questions, I see an aspect of me that doesn't know how to be a parent; that maybe doesn't want to be grown up at all. This part doesn't want to be responsible for another human being 24/7. I see how my child is just reflecting my obstinate, resistant child, unwilling to do what I don't want to do.

I practice accepting my humanness, my desire to do what I want, when I want. I practice accepting who I am in my role as parent. In the best interest of my child,

I practice conscious presence with my child. I experience gratitude for their persistence to wake me up from my sleeping grownup.

Experience #15

Opening to Cultivating Intelligence

True intelligence is utilizing my ability to think and act in alignment with my highest wisdom. Thinking about what I think, and feeling what I feel about my feelings, helps me to grow my intelligence and know myself better.

Recognizing what has me think and feel the way I do empowers me to think differently and feel differently, if I want. Through this practice of being mindful of what I think and feel, I expand my abilities to think and feel beyond what I thought was possible.

Experience #16

Opening to Accepting and Allowing

Human beings are so much more than what I assume, expect, or what I think I perceive. When I practice seeing people as their essential selves, clearing them of the projections I cast upon them, I witness them as being the best they can be. I discover a newfound ability to feel compassion for them, and for myself, as we all face the challenge of revealing ourselves to ourselves.

Experience #17

Opening to Allowing
My Children to Flourish

Though I dearly love my children, I don't always like them. It never occurred to me that I would feel this way. I thought that my parenting would influence them to think and be more like me. I thought my loving presence would override any and every challenge we faced together. Now I see that they are unique individuals with personalities and beliefs that may not match my own. It sometimes feels like they are strangers!

I see that my assumptions and expectations of parenting have been misleading. Now, in the midst of the inevitable truth of my circumstances, I'm invited to think differently. I see that my current hopes, dreams, truths, and values prevent me from experiencing my children as the gifts that they are.

I practice noticing when I'm judging my children for being different from my expectations. I practice surrendering my expectations of who they should be, and begin to accept who they are. I allow myself to be with the sadness that comes when I grieve the loss of my dream-child and our relationship as I imagined it. In so doing, I can begin to accept and appreciate this amazing and beautiful human being, my child.

Experience #18

Opening to Testing My Reality

Personal and spiritual growth requires me to test myself: my thoughts, my beliefs, my actions, and my truths. I won't know my fullest potential unless I nudge myself out beyond those specific thoughts and beliefs that have limited me thus far. Through this practice I realize there is more to me than meets my eye.

Experience #19

Opening to Cultivating Self-Awareness

At any given time in my evolution, I am doing the very best I know how to do. I can only change what I'm aware of. If I'm not aware of it, I can't do anything about it.

I practice being curious, staying open to seeing things differently and suspending self-judgment. And, I allow myself to change my mind when it makes sense to do so.

Experience #20

Opening to Forgiving with Compassion

As a parent, I have made mistakes - some that are unforgivable. I'm crushed by the burden of guilt I carry for being a "bad" parent. I think I'm an unforgivable human being and am unworthy of love.

I watch myself parent out of guilt and realize that this isn't providing good parenting for my children, either. It seems like nothing I do works, and I'm afraid of making even worse mistakes and wrecking my children's lives.

When I stop trying so hard, when I give myself some quiet time, I begin to practice humility, not humiliation; self-compassion – not self-abuse; and I begin to practice forgiving myself for being me.

Though I desperately desire my children to forgive me, it makes sense that I practice doing whatever it takes to forgive myself first. The very act of forgiving myself demonstrates to my children that they can learn to be forgiving of their mistakes too.

Experience #21

Opening to Being Daring

There is a bit of an art to pushing limits and boundaries – I might get in trouble! When to push and how much to push is something I practice, experimenting with what is; expanding into what isn't yet.

As part of this practice, I ask myself the questions: *What is it I'm wanting, enough that I'm willing to push limits? How much trouble am I willing to get myself into? By the way, what is trouble?*

Experience #22

Opening to the Guidance of Universal Wisdom

The practice of believing in myself allows me to open to Universal Guidance in every moment, from everywhere, always. Through this practice, I realize that I am never without support, and I am never left alone.

Like inhaling a breath of life, I open to the ever-present Universal Wisdom and receive the guidance I need. I trust it will be given when I am open to receive.

Experience #23

Opening to Self-Balance

Sometimes, for the sake of productivity and meeting the demands of other people, I ignore signals of my own human needs. Sleepless nights, stress related disease, and a lack of functioning of normal human desires, are consequences of putting my own needs second, third, or fourth to others'.

Instead of automatically fulfilling other people's needs, I practice acknowledging and honoring the needs of my own body, mind, and soul.

Experience #24

Opening to Courage, Conviction, and Self-Trust

Playing small keeps me safe. Playing safe keeps me small. What is safe, anyway? When I practice pushing against my self-imposed limitations, I cultivate courage, conviction, and self-trust. I know, without a doubt, that as I expand into my fullest potential, I will be okay, no matter what.

Experience #25

Opening to Humility and Tolerance for Disappointment

Losing doesn't mean that I've failed, that I'm incompetent, or that I'm inadequate in any way. Losing only shows me the level at which I've achieved success. It lets me know I have a new challenge ahead of me!

When I'm willing to lose, I challenge myself to practice building self-trust, humility, and an ability to be with disappointment, without self-attack or despair. Personal development takes stamina and courage, indeed.

Experience #26

Opening to Gratitude, Courage, and Strength

I'm always at choice to either be upset about my circumstances and predicaments, or to be grateful and appreciate them. Each situation is an opportunity to gather all my daringness and to bring the culmination of all I have to give to this one moment.

I practice seeing life and all the circumstances that are heaped on me, as all good, even when it sucks. I practice being grateful for the way that it is, living in faith, that even the most challenging situations provide a necessary learning, which often is experienced as an incredible gift.

Opening to Accepting the Way It Is

I sometime make decisions for my children that they vehemently reject, and yet I know it is in their best interest to choose as I choose. Sometimes, they don't like me much, and withhold their affections. I then wonder whether I chose correctly, given the current state of affairs.

By considering my choices and how they aligned with what I truly believed to be in the highest good for my children, I feel incredibly hopeless that any decision could be a right decision. I'm left alone with myself, wishing things could be different.

I practice acknowledging myself for having the courage to make the choices I made, and honor myself for acting in the highest good of my children. I respect myself for having taken the high road, even though others perceive that I've done the opposite.

I practice surrendering my will for things to be different. I accept my children's reactions as theirs. I accept mine as mine. And, when I doubt myself, I practice allowing Divine Wisdom to hold the space when I don't know what to do.

Experience #28

Opening to Self-Appreciation,
Self-Honor, and Self-Acceptance

Defeat means I've pushed myself to my limits, exhausting my means to fulfill my desired results, in this moment.

I'm willing to practice pushing the edge of my comfort zone, perhaps meeting defeat every step of the way; all the while experiencing the expansion of who I am within the experience of defeat. In doing so, I daringly face my humanness, and practice self-acceptance, self-honor, and self-appreciation.

Experience #29

Opening to Forgiveness and Self-Compassion

I'm given plenty of opportunities to feel deep disappointment and loss, as well as the heights of joy, and deep love. It's part of being human - experiencing the fullness of all my emotions. It's why I've come to Earth, into this human form.

Emotional moments allow me to know the human side of myself. They allow the fullest expression of ME – my highest of my highs _and_ the parts that I've judged as shadowy, dark, bad, or negative. It's all ME, in all my glory, as Miraculous Existence (ME).

In so practicing, I touch into a level of self-acceptance, self-compassion, and forgiveness that I never considered to be of any real importance. Now I know different.

Experience #30

Opening to Risk, Courage, and Imagination

Dreaming and imagining the most favorable outcome – even those that seem inconceivable, brings me closer to my fullest potentiality.

I practice thinking differently, dreaming bigger, and I allow my imagination to run wild. When I believe in myself enough to take on this practice, I have access to everything I need to manifest my dreams.

Experience #31

Opening to Living Boldly

The World is full of surprises, splendor, and awe. How I choose to see the world either limits me or allows me the fullest experience of LIFE.

When I practice training my mind to look at what is true, enlarging my interpretations of my world to include a more expanded reality, I give myself the gift of a greater capacity to enjoy the exquisite wonder and magic that always surrounds me. I reveal a greater reality within which to live boldly and daringly - as myself.

Experience #32

Opening to Choosing Well-Being

I often feel torn between giving my children quality time and giving myself quality time. Sometimes I'm overwhelmed with so many responsibilities.

When I take a moment to pause and be still, I experience a desire to just be. I practice taking time out for me. I practice turning off all my distractions - phones, electronics, music, TV, and just sit. In so doing, I feel refreshed and available to my child in a way that allows both of us to enjoy our time together.

Experience #33

Opening to Being Curious

Wondering about who I am, what I am, and why I am, is essential to being *all* that I am. I see how I limit my potentiality, and the potentiality of others, when I won't allow myself to see things differently. When I explore, and practice curiosity - questioning reality, I savor and delight in the outrageous answers that come forth in this openness.

Experience #34

Opening to Surrendering the Past and the Future Realities

Looking at the world with fresh eyes & ears, and a beginner's mind, allows me to continually be present to the truth of *this* moment. Building what-ifs, based on my fears of what was, and my hope of what will be, slows me down, or, more often than not, brings me to a full and complete stop.

I practice letting go of how I think my world should look, and I open to being in the reality of today. I suspend my need for this moment to be different.

Opening to Seeing Things Another Way

The world is often incongruous with what I want to believe to be true and real. By practicing acceptance for the way that it is - the diverse people, cultures, beliefs, and behaviors, I grow my ability to see that there are countless ways to be in the world.

I practice sitting and being with conflicting views, and open to seeing things another way. In doing so, another way inevitably shows up.

Experience #36

Opening to Being in the Big Fat Be-With

There is an incredible amount of insanity in this world. When nothing makes any sense, it's just a big-fat-be-with. There is nothing to do and nowhere to go.

I do know, however, that there is sanity beyond what appears to be insane. There is a way to thrive and flourish, regardless of my big fat be-with circumstances.

I practice expanding my capacity to just be-with what is, and I allow the highest truth and the highest goodness to be revealed. Only through this practice will I be able to accept and make sense out of the most exasperating, insane situations. Then, and only then, will I experience peace and serenity.

Experience #37

Opening to Being
the Change I Wish to See

I keep telling my children how important they are to me, even though I have to answer phones, texts, and emails while I'm with them. I don't think they believe me. In fact I notice that they are now answering their phones, emails, and texts when they are with me. I feel more and more insignificant in their lives – and they aren't even adolescent yet.

I now see how my children are a reflection of me, even in all the ways that I cannot see directly. If I don't like what I see in my children's behavior, perhaps I need to shift or consider shifting something in myself?

I practice bringing my actions in alignment with my words. I turn off my phone and other electronics to be present to my children – actually meaning what I say and saying what I mean. In doing so, I'm demonstrating what being present to another person really looks like and feels like inside.

Experience #38

Opening to Going Insane
(But Not today)

What is it like to feel insane? I don't know. I won't let myself feel insane, because I'm afraid that if I feel insane, I'll never feel sane again. I'd rather distract myself from feeling what I feel, especially insane.

However, when I practice allowing myself to at least admit that I'm feeling what I'm terrified to feel, I'm on the road to knowing and accepting me and my feelings for what they are. This thought allows me to see the sanity in admitting the insanity.

Experience #39

Opening to Surrendering

Sometimes I don't know what to think or how to be with what is. When it's just a big fat be-with, again, when nothing but the unknown is present, all there is to do is practice letting go, surrendering my need to understand, my need to control, and my need to manage my circumstance.

Sometimes, nothing is all there is to do.

Experience #40

Opening to the Shining Truth

Sometimes I don't know what to decide, because, as often happens, my desires conflict with one another. When I practice patience and acceptance of how it is, in this moment, decisions often make themselves.

Patience, allowing, and openness to the unfolding of what is, is good. Inevitably my highest knowing and my highest truth will shine forth, and the choice will be self-evident. Don't just do something – Stand there!

Experience #41

Opening to Suspending Control

Rarely can I figure out how the Universe is thinking. That's because the Universe has infinite intelligence – we humans do not. Sometimes the best I can do is to voluntarily suspend control, worry, fear, judgments, and frustration.

When I practice letting go of my attachments to how I want it to be, what inevitably shows up is often far more amazing than I could ever imagine on my own.

Experience #42

Opening to Being My Art

I've been told I cannot make a living as an artist, a writer, an athlete, or a musician. What choices are open to me when it looks like there are none?

When I practice "Be the Exception," and "Go for the Extraordinary," I stop limiting my potentiality. My practice is to allow myself to live into the greatest possible outcome, being the fullest expression of myself, as my art. This thought excites my spirit. I aspire to be my art everywhere in my life!

Experience #43

Opening to Remembering ME

When being ignored by people, I feel invisible and perhaps alien in my surroundings.

I practice knowing that, no matter what, I cannot *not* exist. I remember that although they may not see me, I see myself. I can't ever disappear out of sight of the Universe, for I am ME (Miraculous Existence).

Experience #44

Opening to Engaging With Failure

I didn't think parenting would be such a huge, life-altering, humbling challenge. Day after day, I feel immersed in a barrage of breakdowns and failures. I sometimes feel dreadfully uncertain of the path in front of me.

My desire is to ignore and avoid this discomfort at all cost. However, this avoidance does not seem to bring me closer to a true experience of competence when I'm faced with failure.

I practice noticing the part of me that lies beneath my past successes, and my expectations of future happily-ever-afters. This practice uncovers the me that is so fearful and powerless in the face of failure. It requires being with exhausting angst, worry, and hopeless resignation.

Underlying these emotions is an un-ignorable and undeniable belief that I will fail to get this right and I will fail to get this done. And, I'm still required to show up to the task of parenting, even with this assuredness that at some point, I will meet failure.

I'm inspired to keep meeting myself in failure, as a practice, until I realize that it isn't me that is failing. I'm provided with the insight that failing is only an interpretation of what is actually an incubation period, within which the potentiality for fulfillment of my human spirit resides.

Within this knowing, I cultivate capacities I haven't yet developed, such as courage, resilience, humility, self-compassion, and faith. I practice resisting the belief that I should have had these capabilities already.

In the midst of standing in failure, I realize that this is where life is lived to its fullest. Success is what is learned within what seems to be the vacuous abyss.

Experience #45

Opening to Giving Myself a Break

Sometimes I don't want to be wise. I want to be self-absorbed and selfish. I don't always have to get it right or practice being spiritual. I can give myself a break, if I want.

I can be selfish, demanding, and entitled to a day off.

Experience #46

Opening to Losing My Baggage

Carrying guilt for regrets, mistakes, and failures in no way contributes to the evolution of my spiritual consciousness. It just doesn't!

I practice learning from my mistakes; then, with humility and with courage, I let the baggage go.

Experience #47

Opening to Giving Up
Sacrifice and Suffering

I never have to sacrifice anything. I can choose to give up one thing for something else, only because I want to, not because I have to.

I feel empowered when I take full responsibility for my choosing. I practice reminding myself that my choices require no suffering and no sacrifice. I'm not a victim to life's dilemmas, only to my thinking that it is so.

Experience #48

Opening to Serenity and the Grace of Self-Acceptance

Suffering, like guilt and shame, does no good. It is a greater contribution to the world to practice emancipating myself from the belief that suffering is noble and spiritual. It is not.

Rather than carrying the burden of suffering for eternity, I practice questioning the self-imposed certainty that I must suffer for any sin I've committed and all mistakes I have made.

I give myself permission to dismantle my self-created cage of suffering. I choose to live in serenity and the grace of self-acceptance.

Experience #49

Opening to Seeing without Judgment

Just because I believe that I am right doesn't make it so. When I suspend self-righteous judgment, I practice seeing the world beyond right, wrong, good, and bad. I expand my ability to communicate with others respectfully honoring them and their point of view. Peace becomes not only a possibility, but an inevitable conclusion to my efforts. I have no doubt about this!

Experience #50

Opening to Being Generous With Myself

Getting and taking is not the end-all and be-all of human existence. This is often realized when love expresses itself through me as generosity. In these moments I know for a fact that there is nothing to lose, for in true generosity, there is no loss.

I practice noticing when my only intention is to get something. In doing so, I face the inevitable dilemma: Do I act from my fear of loss? Do I act from my fear of having no power to get what I believe I need? Or, do I choose to trust in the abundance of who I am?

Through this practice of noticing my desire to get, I choose to face the unavoidable discomfort of stretching my capacity to give.

Opening to Presence and Deep Listening

I often forget to put my listening ears on, especially when I'm alone with myself. This may be when I need my listening ears more than ever.

I practice bringing my presence – my full attention to what is in this moment. The practice of deep listening opens me more fully to receive the gifts of this moment. I let my desire to be distracted wait for a later opportunity.

Opening to Being with the Spiritual ME

Spiritual isn't something I do. Spiritual is what I am. I am never *not* Spiritual. Being in conversation with ME allows an awareness that there is something ineffable that is calling. I find myself wanting to peer into a knowing I can't yet know.

I practice stretching and strengthening my courage to see beyond what has been safe for me to see. I willingly sit in the big hairy, scary question that can only be answered by me: Who Am I?

Experience #53

Opening to Being Authentic with My Children

I see that my desire to *look like* a perfect parent is different than my desire to *be* a perfect parent. One way strokes my ego and the other nurtures both my children and my heart.

I practice noticing when I act out of obligation to look like a good parent and use my children for my own motives. I begin to create quality time and presence with them, because that is what I truly desire to experience with them.

Experience #54

Opening to Standing Strong and Loving Strong

The only way I can set strong boundaries with others is to first set a strong *inner* boundary within me, which declares: Here is My Truth!

I can set strong boundaries and limits while still being loving and kind. Sometimes, practicing love through boundary setting is the most loving way to be me.

Experience #55

Opening to Being Content
Within My Own Skin

When I'm restless, irritable and discontent (RID), it is important for me to sit quietly with myself. I practice feeling deeply into the root source of my restlessness, my irritability, and my discontent. This way, I come to uncover choices I've made in the past that generates emotional and physical discomfort.

I open to choosing differently. In doing so, I breathe a sigh of relief and invite in experiences of contentment, humor, joy, and peace.

Experience #56

Opening to Trust and Surrender

I see my children making the same mistakes I made when I was young. I want to protect them and keep them from having to be with the consequences of their own choice-making.

They seem to resent me when I intervene, telling me that I'm being controlling. I know I am being controlling yet, when I stand back and say nothing, I feel defenseless and powerless. I don't want them to have to be with consequences of making mistakes: loss, humiliation, or feeling like a failure and an idiot.

I practice holding my desire to rescue in check. I practice trusting, respecting, and believing that, no matter what, my children are growing themselves up in the way that supports their highest good and highest truth.

Experience #57

Opening to Cultivating Awareness of How I Choose

I can choose to empower myself to do my best, and I can choose to empower myself to do less than my best. I can empower myself to choose to choose whatever I want to choose.

I practice noticing – just noticing, how I choose what I choose. In doing so, I empower myself to choose to open to my highest good, my highest knowing, and my greatest contribution to the world.

Experience #58

Opening to Peace, Love, and Connection

People who act badly are asking for love. They are afraid to ask in a clearer, more direct way.

When I practice being open to listening and hearing their request for love and answering them with love, I experience much less stress and much less strife. I effortlessly enter into peace, love, and connection.

Experience #59

Opening to the Truth in ME

I can't know what truth is for me without the direct experience of it. Reading about it, talking about it, or thinking about it perhaps points me in the direction, but without direct experience of my truth, I remain disconnected; feeling lost, empty, and without direction.

When I practice diving deep, immersing myself in the experience of my truth, I emerge with a knowing that I've never had before. I feel grounded, content, and whole. I am embraced by my truth.

Experience #60

Opening to Discovering the Life Within

Sometimes the noise in my head is so loud I cannot hear a word I am saying. The channel to my inner wisdom is buried beneath mounds of resistance to change. I feel helplessly hopeless. It seems impossible that I will ever get to the essence of ME.

My practice is to purposely engage my listening, and breathe into my desire to know my deepest truth. I then begin to listen for signs of life within, which so desires to be heard.

Experience #61

Opening to Laughing at My Self-Importance

I find it funny that I take myself so seriously, and I laugh out loud when I realize all the silly ways I pretend to be important.

I practice noticing how I can empower myself to separate ME from my foolishness, my insincerity, my pretentious, and my righteousness. I laugh out loud when I look at myself perhaps as God looks at me: with tender love for the innocence that is and forever will be. I delight in my silliness.

Experience #62

Opening to Serenity and Gratitude

Sometimes, I am powerless over my circumstances, and I'm powerless to feel anything but powerless. Attempting to manage, deny, avoid, and distract myself from experiencing this most fundamental experience of human existence is futile. I can be angry, I can medicate myself, I can blame and shame myself and others for the circumstances at hand, but none of these practices will remove the source of my turmoil.

I can, instead, consider the practice of acknowledging when I feel powerless. I can consider the practice of allowing the reality of my powerlessness to just be, only because I'm human and cannot know how to be competent in all areas of human existence. And, I can begin to allow myself to feel more deeply into my humanness, which is within this moment of powerlessness.

I accept that because I am, I will on occasion have no control over me, others, or my circumstance. I can begin to honor myself and all beings for the undeniable existence of powerlessness. As I engage in this practice and I surrender resistance, compassion and serenity somehow mystically appear in its place. And, I find myself grateful for the way that it is.

Experience #63

Opening to Letting Go of Everything that isn't Me

I used to want to be just like my parents. Then, I wanted to be *nothing* like them. Today I am open to allowing me to be who I am, similar to my parents in some ways, and very different in others.

I practice letting go of who I'm afraid I may become and I practice accepting myself as I am. At the same time, I practice choosing to become more of who I always wanted to be, no matter who that may be like.

Experience #64

Opening to Me Without Pride and Prejudice

Each blow to my pride, each disappointment I endure, provides an opportunity to experience the ME beyond the prideful, entitled, fearful person that I thought was me.

I practice distinguishing those thoughts and interpretations, which have me think myself to be wounded and suffering, from those thoughts that I *willingly* nourish; that I'm willing to disappoint others in service to opening to discovering my greatest potential.

I want to model this for my children. These practices nurture humbleness, self-acceptance, and an increasing contentment within me.

Experience #65

Opening to My Paradigm Shift

The dismantling of my personal paradigm, which has always focused on fear, can be profoundly challenging and uncomfortable - physically, emotionally, and energetically.

With ongoing life experiences, I see that I am bombarded by contradicting sensations and thoughts, which I used to accept since "that's just the way life is." Now, I see that these sensations are only indications that it is time to practice mindful consideration of what is true and what is in alignment with my highest good.

As challenging and uncomfortable as it is to sit in the midst of a paradigm shift, I practice allowing myself to feel more empowered to truly be in control of my own evolution. I can go as fast or as slow as is right for me.

Opening to Honoring My Children and Myself

Initially, I wanted children so I'd never feel alone or lonely. They would be my companions for a lifetime. They would become what I always wanted to be, doing what I wanted to do, having what I always wanted to have. The truth is, they are traveling a different road than mine, with different life lessons and life purposes.

This brings me to that which I've attempted to avoid - my aloneness. Over time, my fears of aloneness are shifting. I practice turning aloneness into solitude. Enjoying the company of my children is now a privilege and not a right.

Opening to Being a Positive Impact

My actions impact my children far greater than my words. How I *be* is a reflection of what I believe to be true.

I practice noticing that my actions are coming from beliefs I didn't even know I had. I practice questioning the truth and relevance of those beliefs, and then begin to create beliefs that now make sense, in regard to what I see as absolute truth and well-being for myself.

Experience #68

Opening to Being the Real Deal

Pretending to be something that I am not lessens my capacity to be who I truly am. The truth is, I believe I have to pretend to be who I am already.

I practice noticing when my body is telling me that I'm being something other than centered, grounded, and wholly me. In so doing, I notice when I'm pretending to feel what I want to feel – not necessarily what I truly feel. I notice when I don't want to do what I believe I'm having to do. I begin to wake up to how much I choose, unaware that I've been choosing all along. Now I can choose more consciously to pretend or to be the real deal – ME!

Experience #69

Opening to Clarity and Ease

Problems arise from conflicting desires, beliefs, and interpretations. The clearer I am about what I want and what I don't want, the more likely I am to act in alignment with what I most want.

I practice looking at my problems and what is causing my problems. I notice my conflicting desires and train myself to discern my highest desires from what is either undesirable or just less desired. I discover through this practice that I experience fewer problems and dilemmas, and more effortless outcomes – most of the time. No Problem!

Experience #70

Opening to Consciously Shaping My Destiny

My assumptions shape my perceptions. My perceptions shape my actions. My actions shape my destiny.

I practice discerning the truth of my assumptions, in relation to what I want. I choose actions that will either bring fulfillment to my heart's desire, or frustration, disappointment, and inevitable sabotage to my plans.

I practice catching my assumptions and train myself to assess their truth and their value in relation to what I want to create. I attend to what follows my assumptions and bring my consciousness to the choices I make. Through this process, I experience more self-confidence, and my choices are taking me in the direction I really want to go! Wha-hoo!

Opening to Honoring My Children in Their Own Evolution

By remembering the experiences of my life as a child, my hopes and fears, and experiences of awe and wisdom, I recollect the knowingness I had about life in all of its wonder. I practice remembering the importance of allowing my children and grandchildren the space to experience their own hopes and fears, their own truths, and the rapture of their own exploration. I practice saying to them *"Tell me more!"*

Experience #72

Opening to Adulthood

Adulthood is far more challenging than I imagined. Not only the responsibility to right-livelihood and to my family, but tending to the complexities of a challenging and ever-changing world.

If it is true that the Earth is perhaps beyond repair, how do I be present to my children's fears and questions? I feel powerless to give them answers that will allow them to feel safe and secure even when life looks so scary.

I practice growing courage in the face of fearful circumstances. I practice being present one day at a time, showing up not in ignorance (ignoring my thoughts and feelings), but being fully present in our current circumstances. This requires that I experience deep, human moments of powerlessness, hopelessness, and despair. This, in actuality, honors the truth of my humanity.

For my children's sake, I'm committed to authentic presence, no matter what!

Experience #73

Opening to Good Grief

How do I talk about death and dying with my children? How do I explain death and loss without it becoming traumatic? The topic is so challenging for me. Whether it's the family dog, the fly on the wall, or a close friend or relative, there is still the presence of the absence of life force to explain to my children. I doubt my children's capacity to be with what is so confusing to grownups.

I see that I want to protect my children from the truth and potential trauma that could occur, so I distract us from the subject when it arises. I feel powerless. I don't know the right words to say.

In this moment, I practice being present to my own responses to losses. I practice perhaps openly allowing myself to feeling my real feelings when I'm experiencing loss and grief: my confusion, my shock, my anguish, my anger, my sadness, my powerlessness, and hopefully my acceptance.

I see how, by allowing the authentic responses to loss, I'm much better equipped to share and allow the experience in my children.

There are no magic words that will protect us from the pain and sorrow that comes with loss. The best I can do is to accept death as part and parcel to life. It is a matter of fact, after all. This in itself, empowers me to be with the challenges that come with this aspect of being human.

Experience #74

Opening to Ending Self-Extinction

All my life, I've hidden my truths below layers of pretentious role-playing. In doing that for decades, I feel the insanity of it, as if I had something to lose by exposing my true identity. I realize how much I've lost by hiding my greatest assets – my thoughts, desires and imagination. I want something more for my children.

Mustering courage and strength to practice revealing my truth is a strenuous task. Engaging with myself and the world I live in, staying grounded in that truth is another thing altogether.

By continuing to pretend to be who I am not, I not only lose out on experiencing an optimal life, but I also set my children up for the inevitable extinction of their own human spirit.

I humbly reveal my lack of self-understanding, and acknowledge my fears of weakness and vulnerability.

As I face myself in the mirror, I practice accepting myself as I am. As I embrace myself in this moment, I open to a deep, abiding self-compassion I had yet to know.

Opening to Giving My Children a Ground of Being

Life can be scary. I see the worry on my children's faces as they see me worry about money, work, and more. When I act as if I feel unsafe, I'm teaching them that there is no solid ground upon which to stand. I live as if there is nothing and no one to trust when the going gets tough.

Although I say that there is a higher wisdom, I don't practice *living* as if I trust that higher wisdom.

Opening to giving myself and my children a ground of being, I practice summoning up courage to expose the source of my fear, and I decide to turn toward the support of a higher wisdom and a stable ground of being.

When I practice living as if support is always there, I feel safe to distinguish the underlying *source* of my fear from the *source* of my higher wisdom. I practice creating incremental shifts, not to pretend to be strong, but to actually live strong within my highest knowing, even when I'm scared beyond my wits.

I practice sharing fierce conversations with my children about how they view their world and how they choose to be with their worldly view. Just by talking with them about this stuff will encourage strength within us all. I have no doubt about that!

Experience #76

Opening to Welcoming Failure Again and Again

I've been trained to see mistakes as failures, and failures deserve punishment. This makes me very afraid, and prevents me from taking unknown risks. I've become constantly vigilant to avoid being exposed as a failure; though, to my knowledge I've done nothing wrong. This fearful cautiousness is not what I want to model for my children. How can I teach them to be fearless in the face of failure?

What if failure is just an indicator that something is missing?

When failure occurs, I practice asking myself these questions: What is to be learned here; what am I not attending to; what is calling me; what am I afraid to face; what am I pretending not to know; what part of me feels safe in failing and unsafe in succeeding?

How can I forgive myself, and provide compassion for myself in the midst of all of this? I have some blind spots in this part of my life, and I want to practice bringing it into the light of knowing.

I clearly see that failing isn't the end of anything; it is only the beginning of a cleaner, healthier relationship with me.

Experience #77

Opening to Cultivating Freedom

At times I feel absolutely imprisoned by my own fear to freely express myself. My thoughts often turn to what others think about me. Sometimes, I listen to what they say and agree with them, even when I don't agree. I'm afraid to share my own truths and opinions. I'm ready to liberate myself from this lifelong pattern of denying my self-truth.

I can teach my children to think their own thoughts, to know what they desire, and to freely express their opinions to me and to the world, only by modeling that for them, with them.

I practice expressing my beliefs and opinions in an honest and neutral way. I also practice listening to my children without criticism or corrections – honoring, respecting and being inspired by their free expression. I practice saying: *"I really want to hear what you think."*

Experience #78

Opening to Speaking My Truth to My Family and Myself

I don't like the way my family members treat each other. Sometimes it feels hurtful and abusive. But it's important to love family.

When I practice speaking my truth to my family, I may feel vulnerable to attack, and they may not like me for what I have to say. However, if I'm sharing because I love them and I love myself, then I know it's the right thing to do.

Opening to Cultivating Self-Reliance

I have a belief that in order to feel safe, I need specific things and people in my life. This makes me rely on what's outside of me for my safety and security.

I practice living my life as if I am complete, knowing that I need nothing outside myself in order to thrive. I practice feeling into and enjoying the experience of trusting that I am my own safety-net.

Experience #80

Opening to Living on Purpose

I've always been told that it's important to make lots of money, but I notice that I'm not happy no matter how much money I make. Living my life with purpose and meaning feels more fulfilling and enriching than focusing on money.

Just as a practice, I allow myself to fully embrace my passions and desires, letting go of those fear-based beliefs that limit the flow of abundance. I practice doing what I love, while cultivating the courage to trust that I am supported completely when living a purposeful life.

Opening to Allowing Solitude

After spending so much time on computers, cell phones, and tablets, being alone and quiet sometimes feels really uncomfortable. I forget how to be with myself, without distractions.

Giving myself time to be alone, even living alone, provides a spaciousness that I may never know when I'm too afraid to experience that aloneness.

Taking on the practice of giving myself quiet time every day allows me to cultivate the capacity to be alone, fully present with myself. I may find that in such solitude, I actually enjoy my own company.

Experience #82

Opening to Discovering the Source of My Irritation

When I feel restless, there is a thought that is tickling me, wanting to get my attention. Rather than ignoring the irritation of the restlessness, I practice curiously excavating this tickling thought, and ask it what it wants. I can then stay present to what is possible to alleviate my irritation.

Opening to Doing Nothing When There is Nothing to Do

Humanness sometimes feels good and sometimes feels bad. Allowing for that, I sometimes feel powerless to make me feel better than I do.

In this moment, I can practice empowering myself to accept what I cannot do; not because I'm incompetent or a failure, but because there's nothing to be done by me, now. Doing nothing is something to practice. This is *something* that I can do.

Experience #84

Opening to My Divine Worth

I know I'm a good person, but sometimes I doubt that I'm a *worthy* person. So I do things to prove I am worthy, even when I'm afraid that I'm not.

As I cultivate awareness, I realize more and more that I don't need to prove myself to anyone, especially to myself.

To live a life that fulfills my human spirit, I practice remembering that because I am a spark of the Divine – Divine Worth is my birthright. It is innate, and unquestionably in every one of us.

Opening to Friendships

I know true friendship: it's when I give and receive freely, not looking to get or take anything from my friends, and they aren't attempting to get or take anything from me.

I practice opening myself up to engaging with all beings as if they are my friends, freely giving and freely receiving.

Experience #86

Opening to Self-Honor

Sometimes I question what is mine to do. I wonder how I came to be committed to doing what seems to be so unfulfilling. I notice that I may be under-valuing who I am.

Fulfilling my commitment to doing what is mine to do, and doing it to the best of my ability is the highest form of self-honor.

I practice remembering that self-honor takes courage to stretch into my commitments; fulfilling them because it is what is mine to do. I build strength by leaning into this practice, regardless of the angst and discomfort I may experience.

Experience #87

Opening to Alignment with the Inconceivable

Expanding into my fullest self can only happen when I truly know that I have far more wisdom, strength, courage, and creativity than I could ever conceive.

Acting in alignment with the inconceivable means that I practice living in faith, expanding beyond my perceived limits, trusting my intelligence, my inner wisdom, my imagination, and my inspiration. This practice cultivates deep, deep trust in myself and in the unknown.

Opening to Respecting
the Views of My Children

I sometimes look to friends, business associates and others for validation. I see *my need* to be significant in the eyes of my peers. I forget that my children are important people too, who reflect respect and trust, or reflect the opposite of that.

When I notice that I'm treating my children with less respect than grownups, I practice asking myself "What are my priorities?"

I practice being the kind of person that would be respected by my children. I remember my conviction to do whatever it takes to help my children soar, then practice being the individual who will make that happen.

Opening to Generosity of Spirit

When I withhold forgiving, I contract and I attack. I blame others for my woes, and distrust that anyone genuinely cares.

I'm afraid that by opening myself up to being generous I will lose something that is important to me. Truthfully? I'm afraid I will lose everything. Living in this state of fear keeps me from being the fullest expression of me in the world.

Giving freely – extending myself openly to the world, is for me, the highest and greatest act of self-expression.

For giving sake, I practice noticing when my resistance to being generous arises. I practice releasing those beliefs that limit me from extending myself into the world. I mindfully attend to that part of me that is afraid of loss and lack, and therefore withholds. When I'm generous in spirit, I experience no lack in my capacity to share myself with the world.

Experience #90

Opening to Choosing Consciously

More than ever before, I trust that Being ME in my fullest potential is my life purpose. This makes me happy, because I now have the capacity to create a life that I'm proud to call mine.

I become more intentional in how I choose what I choose. I practice choosing consciously and opening to my highest knowing. By doing so I experience more of my core strength, courage, and power. This inevitably leads me to being the fullest expression of my potentiality.

Experience #91

Opening to Allowing a Wonderful Life

Most mornings, I wake up anticipating the flow of the day as it has been every other day before. This leaves me with the results of my expectations, and therefore the results of my past. And, I wonder why does the "same old, same old" keeps showing up the way it does. I want a wonderful life!

The practice of allowing today to be different pulls my mind back out of expecting and assuming. I stop myself from jumping ahead – thinking about all of the items on my agenda. I practice doing it differently.

Just for today, I *allow* myself to experience life as an unfolding of wonder and delight. I allow myself to be in the moment, practicing presence to life itself. I allow myself to be full of wonder as life unfolds before me. I see there is very little I need to do to allow my life to be wonderful. It just is!

Opening to Discovering Myself in Silence

I find myself afraid of silence. It's uncomfortable. Generally, I locate myself in relation to the noise and stimulation around me. I intentionally bounce from one to another distraction in order to avoid being with ME. If I stop creating noise, I'm afraid I will disappear into an abyss of silence.

As I explore the qualities of silence, leaning into it, I practice listening beyond my limited perception of silence. I actively engage in a process that up until now I feared was a huge vacuum, which sucked me out into the ethers. Through this practice, I discover a richness in the sounds beyond the sounds. Unless I make the leap, I won't know what I may be missing. Who knows, I may even like it!

Experience #93

Opening to Returning to Source

What exists within stillness? Is it the creation of the trees and stars, the ocean and mountains? Is it the source of beauty, love, compassion, and sweetness of a moment of innocence? It takes courage for me to step into stillness – I am afraid that there is something I will lose there. Death-defying? Yes. And perhaps life-giving at the same time.

I practice returning to source by creating moments of stillness for myself.

Experience #94

Opening to the Divine Embrace

With wisdom and maturity, I've come to see that, who I thought I was, as a person, is actually a spark of the Universal Divine. As I surrender my identity and need for my control, I experience the effortless flow with life as it exists in this moment. I practice sensing into the limitless acceptance of the One that embraces me, as the presence that I am.

Experience #95

Opening to Being Out of My Mind

I notice that I often I jump to conclusions about a situation, even before I actually know what it's about. I'm only reacting to my interpretation and my assumption, not to the circumstance which triggered it. "I know what this is about," are the words which keep me from actually knowing anything.

My involuntary judgments and preconceived expectations prevent me from being present to the actual experience of myself in relation to people, places, and things. I'm only experiencing a reaction to my own thinking – nothing more. In this place, there's no room for learning, for wonder, curiosity, or awe. There is no room for direct-engagement with life itself. I miss so much of life by living only in my mind!

I practice noticing when I jump to conclusions. I practice slowing down my responses, empowering myself to be with the real event in real time. In this way, I remain grounded in this moment, where I can truly be with what is.

Opening to Making Room for Me, Now

Though I know theoretically *that there is nowhere to go and nothing to do*, my mind continually races ahead. It believes there is something more important to be doing than what I'm doing now. From one "important" detail of my life to the next, and then to the next, and then to the next. No matter which one I attend to, I anticipate the next to be better than the last. I notice that I get restless when I'm not leaping forward toward the next best thing.

I'm leaving no space for *this* moment. I'm leaving no room for me to be engaged and present to what I am with, in *this* moment. My creations, which only occur in the present moment, cannot come to fruition unless I trust that this is what I am to be with *now*. I have to believe that the fulfillment of *this* moment can only contribute to fulfillment of my larger vision.

While anticipating the voice that says "Let's move on," I practice getting to know myself as I expand my ability to attend fully to the details of now.

As I watch my mind attempt to pull me towards something else, I invite my mind instead to stay present. In so doing, I experience a rapture and delight that exists only in the now, only within the fullest expression of myself, which can only happen in the present moment. That's just the way it is!

Opening to Engaging with the Adventures of My Life

Vicariously accepting the world through other people's experiences is like reading the menu without actually tasting the food. Only through direct experience and personal engagement will I know *my* true experience of adventures available to me in this lifetime: the smell of a rose, my first kiss, my child being born, getting behind the wheel of a car for the first time – no one can live those experiences for me. In these inexplicable moments, I experience oneness with life and a yearning to know *me*, more fully than before.

I practice embracing all that my life offers me. I practice building my courage to step daringly into my life – no matter how frightening it seems. I want to know me through my own experience of me.

Experience #98

Opening to Big Love

There is personal love, which makes me feel special, safe, and secure. Then there is BIG LOVE, which goes beyond life itself, as an expansive, all present, universal, unconditional state of being. Yeowee!

In BIG LOVE we are all the same. There is no prejudice, bias, bigotry, sexism, or racism; BIG LOVE excludes no one.

I want all of us to return to this innate state of being – for it is our Divine Birthright. What if we embraced that which is all embracing? The absolute experience of this embrace is here, right now.

If nothing more, I want to experience just a touch of this BIG LOVE. I want to know what it is like to truly be in the embrace of BIG LOVE. I want to find out how much JOY I can stand. I want to discover all the ways to sustain BIG LOVE through my days.

Today, I practice noticing how I limit my capacity to be love and be loving. I see that every moment is an opportunity to be BIG LOVE. I notice when I miss and dismiss these BIG moments.

I practice sustaining these moments when I am the spontaneous expression of BIG LOVE. Over and over again, I practice re-membering this quality of BIG LOVE in my being. My actions will effortlessly be an extension of BIG LOVE, which I am being.

Experience #99

Opening to Knowing Through Discerning

All I do, all day long, is think about how I'm going to handle life's situations.

I see when:

• I choose to do what I'm told to do, without questioning,

• I choose to resist doing what I'm told to do, and do something else – something I want to do,

• I choose to consider other people's points of view, for their potential values and contributions.

Am I open or resistant? Am I engaging or withdrawing? Am I curious or shut down?

It is up to me to pay attention to how I choose what I choose, so that I can choose in service to my highest knowing. It is up to me to discern what I fearlessly believe to be true, so much so that I am willing to act in alignment with what I believe, and not what I am told to believe.

I practice noticing my bodily responses when other people are sharing their opinions and thoughts. I practice tuning into the quality of these bodily signals, being curious about their message. I practice listening to my inner voice, realizing, with delight, that I'm always receiving trustworthy signals, messaging, and direct, clear guidance of my Divine Truth.

I practice listening to myself with greater respect and honor, for my way of seeing the world is respectable and honorable.

Experience #100

Opening to Living a Blessed Life

Blessings are the bestowing, sharing, and gifting of love and light. These emanate through each of us as wisdom and intelligence of Divine proportion. Through prayers, blessings, and good wishes, I practice living a life of expansive abundance, within which the more I share, the more abundance is in-turn shared with me.

Experience #101

Opening to Self-Discovery

It takes a hell of a lot of courage to practice Self-discovery. It requires me to engage the muscles of allowing, accepting, exploring, and experimenting, This inevitably leads me to leaps of faith, which I wouldn't otherwise take. It requires that I tune in and trust my Divine Guidance.

This practice is an ongoing integration of the absolute truth, which is that we are Spirit, living this human experience. As I practice living in fulfillment of this truth, my children automatically receive the benefits of the wisdom I gain.

I see how my dedication to making my children's spirits soar has brought about my own capacity to take flight. I am free to roam about the Amazingly Divine, Crazily-All Loving and All Giving, Ever-Unfolding Universe!

What could be better than that!

A List of Experiences
to Cultivate in Your Children

Please note: The numbers (#) correspond to the Experience #, not to the page #.

Abundance: #80, 100

Acceptance: #7, 14, 17, 28, 35, 38, 40, 62, 73, 74, 83, 94

Allowing: #16, 17, 19, 40, 42, 62, 65, 71, 73, 80, 91

Allowing Support and Guidance from my Higher Power: #22, 27, 75, 94, 99, 101

Authenticity: #72, 78

Commitment: #6, 72, 86

Compassion: #16, 20, 29, 44, 45, 62, 74

Conscious Choice-Making: #13, 27, 32, 47, 55, 56, 63, 70, 90, 99

Courage: #4, 10, 24, 25, 26, 30, 38, 44, 46, 52, 72, 74, 80, 86, 97, 101

Curiosity: #6, 19, 21, 33, 82,

Direct Experience of Humanness, Truth & Higher Self: #60, 73, 75, 77

Discernment: #13, 53, 59, 64, 68, 69, 70, 75, 99

Discipline: #6

Expansion: #24, 28, 31, 36, 49, 81, 87, 89, 91, 95, 100

Fearlessness: #42, 76, 92

Forgiveness: #29

Giving Up Guilt: #20, 46, 48, 62,

Generosity: #50, 85, 89, 100

Grace: #48

Gratitude: #26, 62

Humility: #8, 10, 14, 20, 25, 37, 44, 46, 64, 66, 74, 95

Humor: #55

Imagination: #30

Innocence: #61, 93

Introspection/Self-Inquiry: #6, 18, 44, 52, 55, 82, 101,

Integrity: #37, 67, 68, 78

Intelligence: # 15, 52

Kindness: #54

Leap of Faith: #41, 44, 75, 87, 101

Love: #50, 54, 58, 78, 98

Mindfulness: #15, 56, 65

Non-Judgment: #16, 17, 19, 49, 95

Openness: #1, 15, 21, 33, 34, 35, 40, 83, 85, 89, 98, 101

Patience: #9, 12, 36, 40, 96

Peace: #7, 36, 49, 55, 58

Questioning Thoughts, Beliefs, and Assumptions:
#68, 69, 70, 79, 80

Presence: #7, 9, 32, 37, 53, 72, 82, 91, 95, 96

Resilience: #44

Respecting Others: #7, 49, 56, 67, 77, 88

Sacrifice and Suffering: #13, 47, 48

Self-Acceptance: #48, 61, 64, 74

Self-Acknowledgment: #23, 28, 43, 62, 74

Self-Appreciation: #28, 61

Self-Empowerment: #15, 42, 47, 56, 61, 65, 73, 83, 95,

Self-Honor: #8, 23, 27, 28, 62, 66, 78, 86, 99,

Self-Respect: #3, 4, 99,

Self-Trust: #2, 24, 25, 79, 87, 101,

Self-Expression: #5, 42, 77, 78, 89, 96,

Self-Worth: #9, 20, 84

Serenity: #36, 48, 62, 83,

Stillness, Deep Listening: #13, 20, 32, 51, 55, 60, 81, 92, 93

Service: #13

Solitude: #7, 66, 81, 92

Surrender/Letting Go: #5, 11, 17, 27, 34, 39, 41, 56, 63, 91, 93, 94

Tolerance: #25

Truth Speaking & Honoring: #4, 8, 54, 72, 74, 77, 78

Wisdom: #94, 100

A Daily
Practice / Prayer / Meditation

I slide effortlessly into my essential truth: that I have nothing that doesn't come from Oneness/Universal Source/God. I surrender my will, my very existence and all its expressions to Oneness. I release any angst and worry that plague me in this moment. I release my judgments, beliefs, assumptions, and interpretations that are not in alignment with my Truth - that which is beyond all right and wrong, good and bad - for I now know that this is where the true nature of life exists. I request support and assistance, not only from wise ones on the planet, but also from the unseens, who are always available. I trust that when I release all thoughts that have me feel angst and worry, my need to control the future and the now will crumble. I know now, through years of experience, that I will be directed very specifically through intuition, inspiration, and perhaps words of the unseen support. I am guided and supported every step of the way.

Reading List

Dr. Seuss: <u>Oh, The Places You'll Go!</u> (1990).

Foundations of Inner Peace: <u>A Course in Miracles</u> (2008).

Peggy Joy Jenkins, Ph.D.: <u>Nurturing Spirituality in Children: Simple Hands-On Activities </u>(2008).

Rasha: <u>Oneness</u> (2006).

Robin Skynner, and John Cleese: <u>Families and How to Survive Them </u>(1984).

Rosie Kuhn, Ph.D.: <u>You Know You are Transforming When… 101 Everyday Indications that You are Creating a Life Happily Ever After</u> (2013).

Rosie Kuhn, Ph.D.: <u>ME… 101 Indispensable Insights I Didn't Get in Therapy </u>(2014).

Rosie Kuhn, Ph.D.: <u>If Only My Mother Told Me: 101 Pearls of Wisdom I Had to Get By Myself</u> (2014).

Rosie Kuhn, Ph.D.: <u>Self-Empowerment 101</u> (2008).

Rudolf Dreikurs: <u>Children: the Challenge</u> (1991).

Tobin Hart, Ph.D., and Joseph Chilton Pearce: <u>The Secret Spiritual World of Children: The Breakthrough Discovery that Profoundly Alters Our Conventional View...</u> (2003).

Acknowledgments

This book has been my most challenging work thus far. It has taken more use of my brain and my will to bring this book into its fulfillment than anything else I've written. Writing is not only about wordsmithing thoughts and imagery into readable and hopefully appreciated sentences; it is also about listening to and transcribing the wisdom of the Universe.

Previous books – such as *You Know You Are Transforming When…* flew onto the pages in a matter of hours – literally. That was pure fun. Conversely, this piece of Divine Wisdom that you're holding in your hand was birthed through arduous labor. Immersed in a constant barrage of failing, uncertain of the path or articulation of what was forming here, I was present to a spiritual practice. This engaged a part of my being, which lays hidden beneath previous ease and success. Angst and despondency, hopeless resignation that I would never get this right and I would never get this done, required that I show up at my desk with the assuredness that once again I would fail.

I learned through my friendship with the fabulous photographer Peter Fisher, that, whether it is our spiritual fulfillment or an artistic one, only through a succession of failings will one penetrate the veils of defeat. Thank you Peter. You inspired me to keep meeting myself in failure, until I realized that it wasn't me that was failing. You provided me with the insight that failing is only an interpretation of what is actually an incubation period; one within which each of us cultivates capacities we haven't yet developed, yet believed we had, or should have.

It has taken the presence of many artists to bring this book to life. As always, Jessica Ruby Hernandez did an amazing job editing the text of this book. I'm so grateful that I can relax and feel confident with her polishing off the final drafts.

Maureen O'Neill, friend and graphic artist extraordinaire transforms texts into poetry. She brings beauty and form to mere words. A deep complex editing process ensued between us, that at times seemed way beyond reason. However the revelations and the clarity that came forth made this book enriching beyond the words and paper it's written on. Thank you Maureen for your incredible wisdom and intuitive gifts.

Deep heart-connecting conversations with Dr. Virginia Erhardt, Carol Anderson, Patrice McAuliffe, David Logan, Marj and Fred Franke, Anusha Solayea, Andrea Shoemaker, brought a refined clarity to my understanding regarding parenting, grand-parenting, step-parenting, and raising all children of the planet. Thank you all for being my friends and confidants.

I am indebted to all beings who have come before me. With the Divine Order of existence, their journeys have brought me to mine. Their fulfillments and unfinished works led me to mine. The interweaving of the past with the present and with the multiple dimensions within which we Earthlings swim, brings me to this moment of realizing – I couldn't do this without them! I am grateful to all!

About Dr. Rosie Kuhn

Dr. Rosie focused her studies in Marriage, Family and Child Therapy in the 80's. In the 90's she specialized in Spiritual Guidance, and received her Ph.D. in Transpersonal Psychology in 2001. In 2000, she began integrating human/family dynamics with transpersonal and spiritual dynamics, creating and facilitating the Transformational Coaching Training Program through ITP, now Sofia University, in Palo Alto, CA.

Dr. Rosie is a preeminent thought-leader in the field of Transformational Coaching. Her interests and passions have taken her from boardrooms to ashrams, in service of supporting every individual to come into the fulfillment of their human-spirit.